PAMUKKALE
HIERAPOLIS-APHRODISIAS

D1337652

R E V A Ş
REHBER BASIM YAYIN DAĞITIM
REKLAMCILIK VE TİCARET A.Ş.

REVAK
PAMUKKALE
HIERAPOLIS-APHRODISIAS

Published and Distributed by
**REVAŞ Rehber Basım Yayın Dağıtım
Reklamcılık ve Tic. A.Ş.**

Photos :
Şemsi Güner, Erdal Yazıcı, Güngör Özsoy,
Halûk Özözlü, Firdevs Sayılan, Dönence Diabank.

Graphic and Layout :
Kemal Özdemir

Typsetting :
AS & 64 Ltd. Şti

Colour Separation and Printed Turkey by
Çali Grafik Matbaacılık A.Ş.

ISBN 975-8212-58-3

R E V A Ş
REHBER BASIM YAYIN DAĞITIM
REKLAMCILIK VE TİCARET A.Ş.

İnönü Mahallesi, Ölçek Sokak No: 172-174,
Harbiye, İstanbul - TÜRKİYE
Tel: (90-212) 240 72 84 - 240 58 05
Fax: (90-212) 231 33 50

P A M U K K A L E

Pamukkale is one of the places in Turkey on which the seal of tourism has been most decisively stamped. No other site in Western Anatolia, not even Ephesus itself, has undergone a process of such rapid change.

Until forty or fifty years ago, Pamukkale was a place where travellers who happened to pass by found peace and tranquillity and the opportunity for quiet meditation by the side of the sacred spring that still lies exposed, amid the few ancient columns and in the deep silence of the tombs that lay scattered over the countryside to the west and extended out towards the surrounding hills. In spite of the doubtful merits of present-day developments, and in spite of all the ugly building construction that has taken place, the seething crowds, the noise and pollution, one can still confidently assert that Pamukkale has lost nothing of its former attractions.

Pamukkalke is located in the Inner Aegean region at a distance of 20 km from the town of Denizli. This lovely, rapidly developing district in the Menderes valley, which enjoys a temperate climate over the greater part of the year, has all the conditions required for an ideal touristic resort.

The tectonic movements that took place in the fault depression of the Menderes river basin gave rise to the emergence of a

Pamukkale travertines.

4

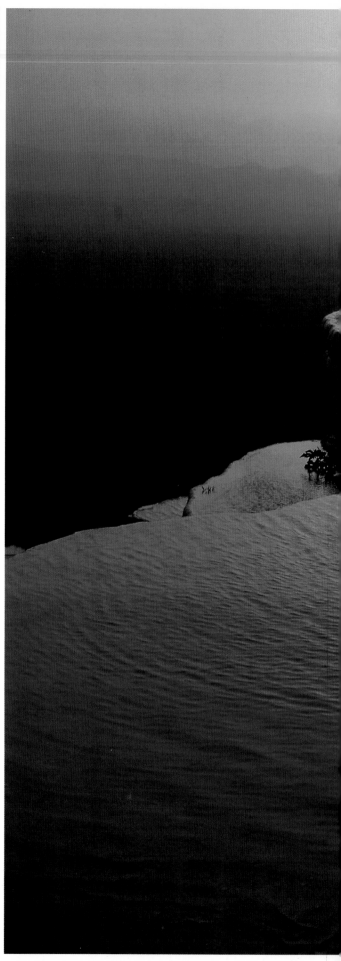

number of very hot springs, and it is the water from one of these springs, with its large mineral content, chalk in particular, that has created the natural wonder now known as Pamukkale, Cotton Fortress or Baumwollenschloss, a very appropriate name for such a phenomenon..

One of the first things to strike you as you make your way over the Menderes plain towards Pamukkale is the fertility of the soil and the amazing variety of the vegetation.

You will also pass by endless expanses of carefully ordered fields of cotton. These fields, so regular that they seem to have been drawn with a ruler, are best seen in spring and early summer.

The months from early summer to the beginning of winter are the season for cotton cultivation and one can never grow tired of gazing on these cotton fields which, even in the hottest weather, seem to be

Two views from travertines.

covered with snow. You may approach Pamukkale by the main roads marked on your map, but there are also other ways, according to the direction from which you are coming. For example, if you approach from the West you can branch off to the left at the sign shortly after Sarayköyü.

This will give you the opportunity of seeing and getting to know quite a few very interesting Western Anatolian villages.

On approaching Pamukkale, whether you choose the route through these villages or arrive by the Denizli road you will be confronted by one of the most remarkable landscapes to be seen anywhere in Turkey.

The first thing you will see is a rock platform over 100 m in height rising up from the plain. The slopes of this hill, which look from a distance like a great white speck, are covered with large numbers of pools and terraces.

As you come nearer, you will begin to see this natural phenomenon, which resembles a frozen waterfall, in greater detail.

From the edge of every terrace and every step in this fascinating natural phenomenon that has gradually formed throughout the ages hang brilliantly white stalactites, and you can hear the joyful

A view from the natural wonder travertines.

Visitors on travertine.

splashing of the waters of the hot springs as they cascade down over slopes where their flow is impeded only by clumps of oleanders.

The temperature of the water forming the travertines, which issues from the hot springs on the hills above, falls to around 33 C^O lower down.

On emerging to the surface, the solution of calcium-carbonate in the spring water decomposes into carbon dioxide, calcium carbonate and water. The carbon dioxide is released into the air while the calcium carbonate separates off from the water to form a greyish-white limestone

sediment.The beds of the water-courses are filled up with these limestone deposits and the water, confronted with these obstacles, splits up into several branches.

The water flows over the slopes into pools, the small basins surrounding them and finally into the fields below.

It is in this way that these terraces over 100 m in height composed of layers of the accumulated limestone sediment have been gradually formed in the course of the ages. As the limestone sediment reaches a certain level the water accumulates in pools and, as these pools fill up, overflows into smaller pools in the vicinity and from these flows

into the small hollows and depressions around them.

The limestone layers in the pools rise up in steps, one above the other, and the continual flow of water keeps this process in operation.

The stalactites form one of the most important features in the landscape. With the formation of the layers and the

Three unique views from travertine.

p.16-17: Views from the ancient pool..

emergence of steps and terraces one above the other, the water leaves the limestone deposit behind it and drips down in the form of stalactites, as in the Damlataş caverns.

The calcium oxide in the water adds to the thickness of the white layers and widens the terraces, producing pools in fantastic shapes reminiscent of oyster shells or flower petals, while the small amount of sulphur and iron oxide produces stripes of yellow, red and green over the white of the limestone.

Any object left in the water at Pamukkale will take on a coating of limestone within a very few days. Now, as in the olden days, the water flows through open channels, and in cold weather you can see columns of mist dancing over the surface.

Although the water flowing from the hot springs on the southern slopes of Çaldağ rapidly loses heat during its flow through these open channels it is still hot enough to make it possible for one to bathe throughout six months of the year in the open-air swimming pools in the motels and on the terraces.

Sunset at travertine.

Multicolour travertine formations in Karahayıt.

HIERAPOLIS

The city of Hierapolis, which was founded on this site in the 2nd century B.C., differs from all other ancient cities in being located, not on earth or rock, but on solid limestone layers formed by limestone water that flowed for centuries over this raised level plateau.

"Hierapolis" can mean "sacred city", and according to Stephanus of Byzantium the city was given this name because of the large number of temples it contained.

Up to the reign of Augustus the city was officially described on coins as Hierapolis, the city of temples, but it seems reasonable to assume that this was not the original meaning of the name.

The founder of the city was Eumenes II, King of Pergamon, and it was the custom for Hellenistic kings to name the cities they founded after members of their own families. It thus seems much more likely that the city was named after Hiera or Hiero, the wife of Telesphorus, the legendary founder of the Pergamene dynasty.

We have no definite records concerning the foundation of Hierapolis, but the tradition that it was founded by the Pergamenes would appear to be reliable. In the middle of the 2nd century B.C. the Seleucians founded the city of Laodicea and, as it would seem extremely unlikely that they would found a second city in such close proximity to an already existing one, it seems reasonable to suppose that Hierapolis was not then in existence and that it was founded at a later date, probably in the first quarter of the 2nd century B.C. The region became subject to the Pergamenes after the battle of Magnesia in 190 B.C. There is no definite proof of the

Views from travertines in Pamukkalee.

existence of a settlement on this site in more ancient times, but it seems u nliklely that such a remarkable site should have been left uninhabited.

The historian Herodotus (5th century B.C.) speaks of a city named Cydrara in the vicinity.

We know that a city named Hydreia, or "rich in waters", synonymous with the name of the modern town Denizli, existed until as late as the Roman period. By that time Cydrara had already disappeared. The written history of Hierapolis begins with the Roman period.

As a result of the transfer of the Kingdom of Pergamon to Rome in accordance with the terms of the will left by Attalos III, Hierapolis came under Roman rule in 129 B.C. as part of the province of Asia. Later records are chiefly concerned with a series of earthquakes.

The city was devastated by an earthquake which took place in 17 A.D. during the reign of Tiberius, but the most severe of all the earthquakes occurred in 60 A.D. during the reign of Nero. The present appearance of the city probably results from the reconstruction after this earthquake carried out with the financial assistance of the Emperor.

No events of note are recorded in the subsequent period apart from visits to the city made by the Emperor Hadrian in 129 A.D., the Emperor Caracalla in 215 and the Emperor Valens in 370.

The city received the much coveted title of Neocoros from the Emperor Caracalla. This accorded the city certain administrative privileges as well as the right of sanctuary.

There were a number of Jewish colonies in Hierapolis with their own more or less independent organizations.

As in the cities of Laodicea and Colossea, Christianity began here at a very early date. The Apostle Philip spent the last years of his life here with his daughter, and was finally buried here.

In the 6th century, the Bishop of Hierapolis was raised by the Emperor Justinian to the rank of metropolitan.

Almost all the names of the city notables to be found on the various inscriptions are Greek or Roman.

The city assembly was composed of Greeks, but the names of the tribes are Phrygian. Religion displayed a powerful Anatolian influence. Most of the Greek gods were worshipped here, but these were usually fused with local deities, providing evidence of the persistence of the cultural and religious influence of the Anatolian peoples who had inhabited the area for thousands of years. Although the Greeks founded a number of colonies along the coast, Hellenic culture penetrated into Anatolia only centuries later following the victories of Alexander the Great and his generals. Both the Greeks and the Romans, who later took over the administration of the region, adopted the traditions of the local population, moulding them into a new form by combining gods with more or less similar functions.

This syncretistic process was by no means unique to Hierapolis. The same was to be found all over Anatolia. Of the gods and goddesses whose statues have survived, the Ephesian Artemis and the Aphrodisian Aphrodite are the finest and most typical examples of this syncretism. In the case of these goddesses, the influence of Anatolia is clearly manifested in their attributes and the various local features they display.

Apollo, the chief god of Hierapolis, was identified with the Phrygian sun god Lairbenus, whose temple was to be found 30 km north-east of the city.

Leto, the mother of Apollo, has been compared to Kybele, the Anatolian mother goddess and, in the same way, Zeus was given the cognomen Bozius or Troius,

A dreamy sunset at travertines.

neither of which is Greek in character. The many deities and temples in the city included a number of temples to foreign deities such as the Ephesian Artemis, while representations of Men, a sun god of Anatolian origin, are to be found on their coins.

Of the purely Greek gods the most important were Poseidon, who was responsible for earthquakes, and Pluto/Hades, the god of the underworld. The importance in which these gods were held can be explained by the frequency of earthquakes in the region and the underground gas and water containing various minerals and compounds which were a characteristic of the region.

It was through these features that Hierapolis won fame in ancient times. Various writers of the period dwelt on the interesting phenomenon known as the Plutonium. Strabo writes as follows:

"The Plutonium is a fissure wide enough for a person to enter. It is very deep. An area of some 30 ft in width surrounded by a fence is covered by a thick mist which makes it impossible to see the actual place. The air outside the fence is quite clear, and when no wind is blowing there is no danger in approaching it, but any living creature who enters dies on the spot.

Large animals that enter the fissure immediately collapse and are brought out as corpses. We sent birds in as an experiment and saw them drop dead immediately on entering. Only the eunuchs of the temple of Kybele are able to spend a short time within the cavern without being affected."

Asclepiodotus, who visited the region in the fifth century, attempted to reach the source of the water by tying a bandage

Two surrealistic views from travertines.

around his nose and mouth and making his way against the flow of the stream, but a sudden increase in the depth of the water prevented him from proceeding beyond a certain point. In the 2nd century it was converted into a tourist centre where food and drink was sold to the visitors. Later, a temple was built here and the site of the Plutonium assumed its present-day appearance.

Various athletic and musical competitions were held in Hierapolis, as in other ancient cities.

Under the Empire, crowds flocked to Olympic, Phyrian and Actian games similar to those in Greece. Strangely enough, there is no trace of a stadium in the city, and it is generally thought that the stadium must have been located on the level plain below.

Gladiatorial combats and wild beast shows were held in the theatre.

But Hierapolis was not only a centre of excursions and entertainment. The city's wealth and importance stemmed from the many and varied industrial establishments to be found there. The inscriptions refer not only to institutions such as the wool industry co-operative but also to guilds formed by the dyers, fullers, carpet-weavers, nail manufacturers and coppersmiths.

These were all associated with fully organized institutions that were also responsible for the care of their members' graves.

Export goods included a type of marble unique to Hierapolis. The quality of this marble and the colour it displayed is said to

Three views from Pamukkale and its environments.

Two views from neighbourhood Pamukkale.

Villagers weaving carpets.

have been due to the effect of the hot spring water on the marble deposits. With only one exception, this marble was never used in any of the buildings in the city itself.

The best known of the city's many distinguished citizens was the sophist Antipater, who was chosen by Septimius Severus as tutor to the future Emperors Caracalla and Geta. The tomb of Antipater's family is located in the north of the necropolis, but his own has not been identified.

The city enjoyed its most brilliant period in the 2nd and 3rd centuries and the presence of a Jewish community facilitated the early spread of Christianity. It was here that the Apostle Philip was martyred in 80 A.D. and the church dedicated to the saint

was largely responsible for the increased importance of the city during the Byzantine period. Other important buildings in the city date from the Late Roman or Early Byzantine periods.

The city recovered from a severe plague epidemic at the end of the 2nd century, and Constantine the Great later honoured the city by proclaiming it capital of the Phrygian region.

For Hierapolis, as for other cities whose administration and commerce were adversely affected by the Crusades and the Mongol invasions, the 12th century was a period of rapid decline.

It was never reconstructed after the devastating earthquake of 1219 and was gradually abandoned to the tender mercies of nature.

THE RUINS

The remains to be seen at the present-day all date from the Roman period. Nothing has survived from Hellenistic times. Even the city defence walls are no exception. These walls are not very impressive in either height, strength or quality. Indeed, there was no need for strong city walls during the period of the *Pax Romana* and, in any case, the sacred character of the city was its most effective protection. The walls were very probably erected against thieves rather than hostile armies. The ruins to be visited include the remains of the city defence walls, the foundations of the temple of Apollo, the site of the Plutonium, the nymphaeum, the theatre, the sacred pool, now incorporated in one of the motels, the Gate of Domitian, the triumphal arch, the Byzantine gate, the colonnaded street, the baths, the cistern outside the walls, the churches, the necropolis (the collection of tombs on the west) and the foundations of the tomb of St. Philip on a hill outside the city. The first excavations on the site were carried out in 1887 by a team of German archaeologists under the direction of C.Humann. A collection of the excavation notes kept by the archaeologists Humann, Cichorius and Judeich was published in Germany in 1889 under the title *Altertümer von Hierapolis*. In 1957, work in this region was begun by a team of Italian archaeologists under the direction of Professor Paolo Verzone. The very successful restoration of the theatre carried out in recent years is the work of these Italian archaeologists. The plan of the city is in the nature of a rectangle with an east-west alignment. The streets are arranged to intersect at right angles, forming rectangular blocks. The streets were reserved for pedestrians, and those running from north to south traversed the whole length of the city. The alignment of the Plateia, the most important street in the city, which cut across the east-west

Two views from Hierapolis.

The city plan of Hierapolis.

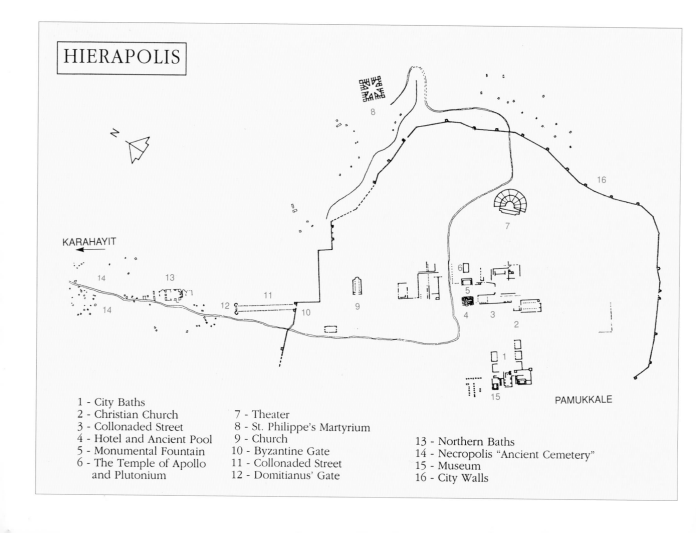

HIERAPOLIS

KARAHAYIT

PAMUKKALE

1 - City Baths
2 - Christian Church
3 - Collonaded Street
4 - Hotel and Ancient Pool
5 - Monumental Fountain
6 - The Temple of Apollo
   and Plutonium
7 - Theater
8 - St. Philippe's Martyrium
9 - Church
10 - Byzantine Gate
11 - Collonaded Street
12 - Domitianus' Gate
13 - Northern Baths
14 - Necropolis "Ancient Cemetery"
15 - Museum
16 - City Walls

colonnaded street, serves to indicate the position of the north and south gates. The north gate is flanked by towers with architectural decorations.

THE NECROPOLIS

If you enter Pamukkale from the western gate, in order to reach the travertines you will first of all have to cross a vast necropolis, offering you a view of the largest and most important cemetery in the world.

The instinct for life has always been the dominating force in all living things. From the earliest times, human being have striven to find cures for the various diseases with which they are inflicted. In doing so they have exploited to the full all possible natural resources and no doubt the hot springs of Pamukkale attracted attention ages before the appearance of the first written records. Most of the tombs belong to the Hellenistic and Roman periods but some of the tomb types date back to very early times, indicating that long before the city of Hierapolis was founded people were coming here to seek a cure in the hot springs.

Those who found a cure undoubtedly returned to their own countries. But what happened to those who didn't? They probably remained here for the rest of their lives and were finally buried here. This is the reason for this vast necropolis that occupies over a square kilometre of the ruins, and for the great variety in the types of tombs to be seen here.

In accordance with ancient beliefs, a gold or silver coin or, sometimes, a coin of electrum, an alloy of the gold and silver, was placed in the mouths of the deceased to serve as a bribe to the boatman who was to ferry them over the river of Hades.

In later times, tomb robbers were to find these coins embedded in the skeletons of the deceased, and, unfortunately, the tombs at Hierapolis, like those in all the other ancient cities, were pillaged by robbers

Views from the necropolis of the ancient city Hierapolis.

from Byzantine times onward. Some tombs, however, which were completely covered by the earth, were still found to contain personal effects such as oil-lamps and tear glasses.

In view of the devastation wreaked by the passage of time, that any of these tombs should have survived to the present day is a real miracle. Most of them were repaired and salvaged by the Italian archaeologists in the course of their excavations.

The variety displayed by these tombs indicates that people came here from all parts of Anatolia.

Undoubtedly, only the wealthiest could erect tombs for themselves, the less well-to-do being buried in graves of which very little trace remains.

Thus, that there should be as many as one thousand tombs in the North-Western Necropolis is really quite amazing.

Most of these tombs are of the sarcophagus type, The manner in which the lids are carved gives a clear indication of the region to which the deceased belonged. The fact that some of them are quite plain while others display ornately carved decoration gives some idea of the differences in social and economic status of those buried within them.

The second large group of tombs consists of house-type tombs. Most of these are still buried under the earth, only the most imposing being visible above ground. It seems probable that these house-type tombs contained several bodies, all probably belonging to the same family.

The third and less numerous category consists of the tumulus tombs consisting of a burial-chamber covered with earth.

Over the centuries some of the earth has been blown away by the wind leaving sections of the burial chamber exposed. These are all family tombs.

A mausoleum squeezed in travertine formations in Hierapolis.

Two typical views from the necropolis of Hierapolis.

THE CHURCH BATHS

Continuing towards the west after crossing the necropolis and having, perhaps, taken a look at the ancient ruins on the left as you approach the city defence walls, you will find yourself confronted by an enormous building on the right hand side of the road. Originally a bath building constructed in the 3rd century during the Roman period, in the 4th century, after the establishment of Christianity as the official religion of the Empire, it was converted into a church, losing all the distinguishing features of a Roman bath in the process. It is now generally known as the "Church Baths" in order to distinguish it from the large bath building now used as a museum.

This extremely imposing building is constructed of stone blocks of a considerable size and weight and, with its vaults and arches, gives a very clear idea of the massive strength of Roman architecture. Unfortunately, it has suffered a great deal of damage from earthquakes and the north wall can be seen to be leaning very precariously to one side .

THE MONUMENTAL WAY and THE ROMAN GATE

Continuing on your way towards the east past the church baths and a small fountain you will arrive at a monumental gate. Passing through one of the three arches you will emerge into the monumental way.

Excavations yielded evidence that in Roman times this road continued outside the gate and was lined with shops. Generally known as the Domitian Gate on the strength of a small inscription on the monumental gate to the effect that it was built by the Emperor Domitian in the second half of the 1st century, it is also sometimes known as the Frontius Gate because its construction coincided with

Views the North Church (Roman Bath).

The gate of Emperor Domitian (Roman period gate).

The gate from Byzantine period.

The gate of Emperor Domitian

A detail from the Byzantine period gate.

Frontius' period of office as proconsul of Asia. The gate is flanked by defence towers in a fairly good state of preservation.

Beyond this point the remains of the city defence walls towards the north are in very poor condition.

As has been pointed out above, all the streets in the city intersect at right angles. In other words, this is an example of the "grid plan" associated with Hippodamos, the famous town-planner of the Hellenistic period.

The widest street in the city is the Monumental Way, a colonnaded street on each side of which one can still see the remains of houses and various other buildings.

The water channels of hewn stone running along each side of the street and branching off to right and left are still in a fairly good state of preservation.

THE BYZANTINE GATE

At the end of the Monumental Way, with its colonnade and water channels on each side, stands another gate in a fairly good state of preservation. This gate, constructed during the Byzantine period, continued to be used as long as the city remained inhabited. Although the defence towers flanking the gate are in ruins some wall fragments are still visible.

In the small area between the Monumental Way and the Byzantine gate, excavations have revealed a structure resembling a forum, where political discussions were once held.

The excavations also yielded a number of columns and capitals of various styles together with fragments with carved reliefs displaying very fine stone workmanship. The remains of a Byzantine church with rooms for the priests and two rows of

columns separating the interior into three aisles can be very clearly seen immediately behind the Byzantine Gate.

THE MARTYRIUM OF ST. PHILIP

The imposing remains of the martyrium constructed in the first half of the 5th century in memory of St. Philip can be seen on slightly higher ground just outside the city defence walls.

The efforts of St. Philip resulted in the foundation here of one of the first Christian communities and one of the first Christian churches. After Philip's crucifixion by the Romans in 80 his son continued the work

A general view and details from St. Philip Martyrium.

Hierapolis, ancient water arks.

of proselytism. Although it would seem reasonable to assume that St. Philip was buried on the site of the ruins of this martyrium no trace has been found of his grave. The martyrium itself is an octagonal structure on foundations measuring approximately 20 x 20 m. Access to the martyrium is afforded by a monumental flight of steps leading up to the building on the side towards the city.

THE CITY DEFENCE WALLS

As the city was in no danger of attack during the Byzantine period the stones of which the walls were composed were carried off by the local inhabitants for use as building material. Thus practically nothing survives of the walls apart from a few fragments in reasonably good condition.

These remains, which are to be found mainly in the area between the martyrium of St. Philip and the theatre, are composed of carefully hewn stone blocks displaying very fine stone workmanship.

Traces of a number of monumental buildings and several gates can be observed on the city side section of the walls extending along the slopes of the mountain, but as in some places no excavations have so far been carried and in others excavations already begun have not yet been completed, nothing definite is known concerning the nature of these structures.

THE ANCIENT THEATRE

The most interesting of all the sites in Hierapolis, after the Pamukkale travertines, is undoubtedly the ancient theatre. Although rather smaller than other specimens that have survived in equally good condition it is well worth careful examination on account of its beautifully preserved marble reliefs.

Although at first glance its location on the slope of a hill gives the impression of a Greco-Roman structure, its method of construction, employing vaults and arches, is typical of the Roman period. Although, according to some sources, it could hold over 10,000 spectators, the most optimistic estimate would give no more than 8,500. Construction of the threatre was begun under Hadrian in the first half of the 2nd century, but was completed only about a hundred years later during the reign of Septimus Severus. The cavea is divided by eight stairways set at regular intervals, with twenty tiers of seats up to the level of the diazoma and twenty-five tiers above it.

The facade of the stage building is an exquisite example of the art of stone-carving and is adorned with carvings in high relief of a very high plastic and artistic quality.

Although these reliefs mainly represent mythological stories related to Apollo, the large number of ornaments in the form of oyster shells are reminiscent of Aphrodite. A large number of the reliefs unearthed during the archaeological excavations carried out in the theatre are exhibited in the local museum in the Roman baths.

The marble artefacts scattered over a wide area in front of the theatre include a number of very interesting masks and other decorative elements.

Hierapolis, ancient theatre.

Views from the ancient stage.

Views from the stage of the ancient Hierapolis theatre.

THE TEMPLE OF APOLLO

The temple of Apollo is located on a slope between the sacred pool and the theatre. The temple, which faces south-west, is reached by a flight of steps. The front of the building rests on a podium 2 m in height while the rear rests on the native rock.

The discovery of this temple of Apollo was one of the most remarkable achievements of the Italian excavation team. The first thing to be revealed in the excavations carried out in the southern section of the remains, which were almost entirely buried under the soil, was the Plutonium, consisting, as Strabo had described it, of a fissure located behind the temple. Here they found a chamber 3 m in size and behind this, flowing out very rapidly from the fissure, there emerged a stream of water giving off a very pungent-smelling gas. The chamber was entered by descending three steps and passing through an arched door. In view of the fact that Strabo, in describing the Plutonium, made no mention of any building, it would appear that the temple must have been constructed at a later date. The temple of Apollo is a comparatively short structure 18 m long and 15 m wide consisting of a pronaos and a cella with, apparently, a row of six columns in front. In view of the fact that the building is largely constructed of spolia and that the site had previously been occupied by an older temple or other building, probably belonging to as early as the Hellenistic period, the present remains cannot be older than the 3rd century A.D. In the course of the excavations it became apparent that the gas rising from the Plutonium caused a certain discomfort. A solution to this was found in ancient times by arranging for the gases to escape at the

sides through 2 inch openings between the blocks forming the foundation of the temple. This expedient is particularly evident on the side towards the podium.

Various inscriptions can be seen on the stone blocks of which the temple is composed. Of these, the one in northern corner of the cella refers to a plague epidemic, probably the great plague which affected the whole of the Empire in the 2nd century during the reign of Marcus Aurelius. As in all such cases, people were strongly advised to offer votive oferings to the gods, and, of course, to Clarus Apollo in particular. An interesting thing here is the following declaration from the mouth of the god: "For you are descended from me and from Mopsus, the founder of the city."

Mopsus, who possessed the gift of being able to foretell the future, was a hero who settled in Claros after the Trojan War (12th-13th century B.C.). Although the idea that a city generally thought to have been founded in the Hellenistic period was in some way connected with a personage who lived in so much earlier a period would appear to merit little credence, it is quite clear that this was a belief generally held in the city itself.

Mopsus is represented on the coins minted in Hierapolis, and he was also connected with Torrhebus, another mythical personage.

Torrhebus is also the name of a city in the province of Lydia and a temple of Carius is located on a mountain nearby. Acording to the legend, the hero Torrhebus learned music from the Muses while walking by the edge of the lake and taught it to the Lydians. (In Greek mythology the nine Muses were daughters of Zeus, and each taught and encouraged various arts such as poetry, dance and music.)

The lake in question lay a little north of

A look to the ancient theatre from Apollon temple.

Pamukkale Museum (Ancient Roman Bath).

the city of Sardis and may very well have been the present-day Gölcük about 100 km north-west of Hierapolis. The citizens of Hierapolis obviously invented for themselves a legendary past that included such personages as Mopsus, Clarius Apollo, Torrhebus and Careius. (As the coins testifying to these connections were minted in the middle of the 2nd century A.D. it would appear that they were in some way related to the oracle in the temple, but, on the other hand, it is significant that the hundreds of delegations to Claros during the Imperial period included not a single delegation from Hierapolis. The worship of Artemis and of Ephesian Artemis in the city is connected with Apollo. Artemis is included in the hierarchy of gods as the sister of Apollo, while in mythology Ephesian Artemis was one of the most powerful goddesses in the region.

THE ROMAN BATHS (PAMUKKALE MUSEUM)

The building in which the local museum is housed consists of Roman baths dating from the 2nd century A.D.

It is in an excellent state of preservation and, with its vaults and arches, displays all the characteristic features and beauty of Roman architecture.

The bath consists of three rooms, now used as the salons of the museum: the caldarium, or hot room; the tepidarium, or warm room; and the frigidarium, or cold room.

To the east of the building lies a palaestra measuring 35 x 50 m where, in Roman times, young people or those of a sportive nature could practise various sports in order to warm up and start the body sweating.

It was also used as a training ground for

athletes, and as a venue for certain ceremonies.

At the present day, the palaestra is used for the exhibition of a number of objects found at various places in the course of the excavations.

Views from the galleries of Pamukkale Museum.

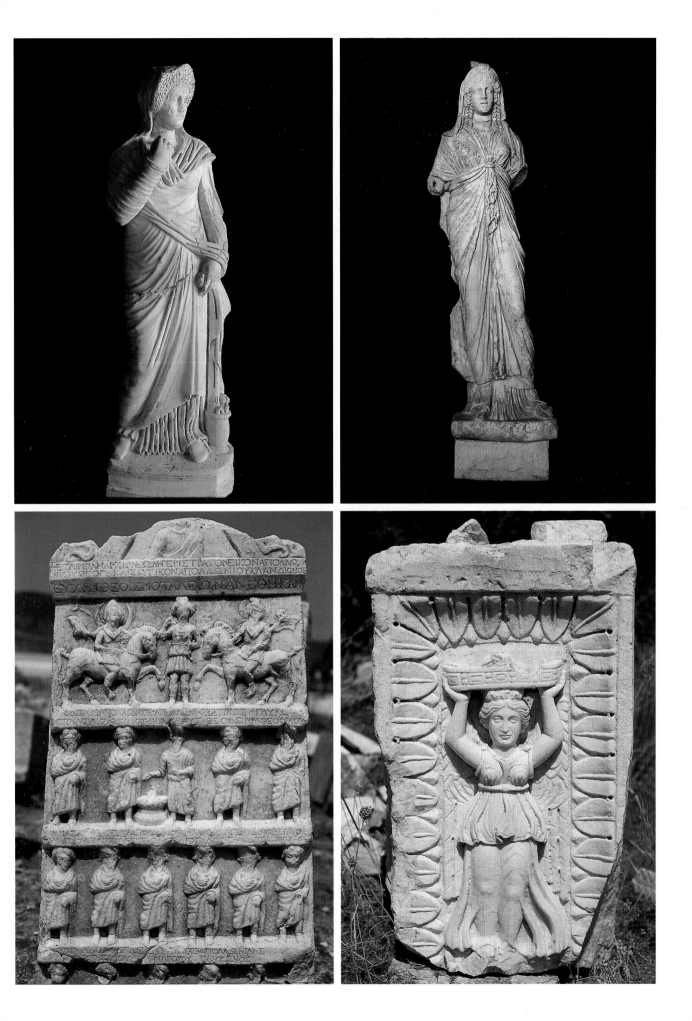

FRAGMENT OF ASARCOPHAGUS OF SIDAMARA
(Roman Period)
SIDAMARA TİPİ BİR LAHT PARÇASI
(Roma Devri)

Various statues and reliefs in the garden of Pamukkale Museum.

p.50: Views from Pamukkale Travertines.

LAODICEA

We fervently advise everyone who is to visit Pamukkale (Hierapolis) to take a close look at Laodicea which lies only 10 kilometers away.

Although there is not much left other than the amphitheater and the monumental fountain (nymphaeum) which have been pretty badly ruined, you will have a chance to see the place where one of the most important seven churches of Christian history used to stand.

The earliest settlements in this area date back to the very old ages but only little proof of those times have been found. Laodicea was founded as a site in the first half of the III. century B.C. King Antiochos II. has founded the city because of its potential political importance in an area which lay just on the border to Caria, and has named it after his queen, Laodicea.

Laodicea fell to the Kingdom of Pergamum in the II. century B.C., and then to the Roman Empire after a short while like the rest of the Anatolian antique cities. It was alternately ruled by the Romans and the King of Pontus, Mithridates, during the wars they fought, and was destroyed by a mighty earthquake in 60 B.C.

Laodicea lay in ruins for quite a period of time but the visit of the Roman emperor, Hadrian, at the beginning of the II. century A.D. led to its revival, and it was almost totally rebuilt during the reign of Caracalla. It flourished by its textile production and stock-farming, and became a rich center for commerce and the arts.

Laodicea grew to be an important religious center at the Byzantine era because one of the most important seven churches of Christianity happened to be there, and it was turned into an archbishopric.

A view from Laodicea ancient city.

Another terrible earthquake destroyed the city at the end of the V. century A.D. It could not be revived again and it lost its former prominence gradually. Especially the growth of Denizli nearby led to the immigration of the natives of Laodicea which was named "Ladik" under Turkish rule. Because the city used to host a big population, it had two amphitheaters.

Only some rows of the seats are to be seen today. It is still possible to witness the former grandeur of these theaters although the stage buildings and other architectural elements have been ruined completely. The monumental fountain which is totally ruined but the pieces of which have been scattered around, looks like it can reappear in its former beauty after a thorough reconstruction.

It is obvious that there has once been a large pool in front of the fountain which has been restored occasionally through the years. The most outstanding monument of Laodicea is the stadium with a length of almost 355 and a width of 65 meters, and which used to be one of the most important stadiums of antiquity.

Although the squared stones of the seats have been carried away by the local population to be used in the construction of other buildings, the remaining parts suffice to give an idea of its original form and size.

Other than these, it is possible to see the ruins of a pretty damaged odeon and another monument which was probably a gymnasium.

The necropolis is at the other side of the river bed that lies to the west of the antique site. Quite a number of mausoleums can still be visited at the necropolis today.

APHRODISIAS

The ancient city of Aphrodisias, once the capital of the province of Lydia, is located near the village of Geyre in the district of Karacasu 38 km south of Nazilli.

In ancient times, the attractive marble buildings of Aphrodisias no doubt shone out, as they do now, from amidst the rich vegetation of the Dandalaz valley with its almond, pomegranate and poplar trees.

The wealth and cultural and political importance of the city is clearly attested by the size and magnificence of the buildings of which it is composed.

The name Aphrodisias is derived from Aphrodite, the goddess of nature, beauty, love and plenty, and was one of the most famous cult centres of the goddess. But this was not the original name of the city.. According to the historian Stephanus it was founded by the Lelegians and was first known as Lelegonopolis.

Monumental theatre of Aphrodisias.

The name of the city was later changed to Megalopolis, and later again to Ninoe after Ninos, the King of Assyria.

The history of the city can be traced back to the early bronze age and there is even clear evidence of a chalcolithic culture prior to the 3rd millennium B.C. The use of the name Aphrodisias began after the 3rd century B.C., in the Hellenistic period..

The spread of Christianity under the Byzantine Empire and the gradual adoption of Christianity as the state religion resulted in a marked change in the status of the city. The cult centre of Aphrodite declined in importance, to such an extent that the names Aphrodite and Aphrodisias were finally erased from all the inscriptions. Efforts were made to change the name of the city to Stavrapolis, the City of the Cross, but the local inhabitants preferred to use Caria, the name of the province. Geyre, the name of the modern village occupying the same site, is probably a corruption of the ancient Caria, which occurred after the

A detail relief from the theatre.

Turkish occupation of the area. It seems very likely that in Turkish, Caria was first of all pronounced Kayra, and that the "k" was then changed to "g" and the "a" to "e". Aphrodisias is located in an earthquake zone and has no doubt experienced innumerable tremors throughout its history, but as, in each instance, the damage was very skilfully repaired, no traces of this damage have survived. On the other hand, very great damage was caused by the flooding due to a change in the level of the underground water table resulting from earthquakes that occurred between 350 and 360. Like several other Roman and Byzantine cities, Aphrodisias was very largely self-sufficient.

Hierapolis was one of the foremost cities of the age, surrounded by fertile fields producing every type of foodstuff. It also possessed a flourishing wool and cotton industry, highly developed commercial, political, religious and cultural institutions, a very fine tradition of arts and crafts, world-famous schools of philosophy and sculpture and a large and energetic body of citizens.

The decline of the city was hastened by an unforunate incident that took place in the 7th century. The reign of the Emperor Heraclius (610-641) was marked by Arab raids and incursions from the East, religious disputes, political and economic pressures and a number of epidemics causing great loss of life, but the final stroke was dealt by a devastating earthquake. The damage caused to the buildings by this earthquake is still plainly visible. Some of the most imposing buildings were destroyed and remained unrepaired.

Very little is known of the history of the city after the 7th century, sources of information being confined to a few religious documents and lists of the names of the bishops. Archaeological finds, however, would appear to point to a short-lived revival in the 11th century.

The incursion of the Seljuk Turks from Anatolia between the 11th and 13th century

Various statues, reliefs and architectural staff in the garden of Aphrodisias Museum.

meant the end of the settlements that had survived the great earthquakes. After the 13th century the whole province became subject to the Aydın and Menteşe Emirates. In the 15th and 16th centuries the fertile soil of the area attracted new settlement and the site of the ancient city of Aphrodisias was occupied by the village of Geyre.

THE REDISCOVERY OF APHRODISIAS

Aphrodisias owed its fame very largely to its school of sculpture. The reason for the choice of this city by the distinguished members of this school lay in the quarries of high quality marble to be found in the vicinity. In the Roman period, the busts, statues, reliefs and friezes exported to the capital of the Empire were so much in demand that Rome decided to invite the sculptors themselves. Very few of the artists of this period signed their works, but, by the 2nd and 3rd centuries, the extraordinarily high regard in which the sculptors of Aphrodisias were regarded removed any qualms they may have felt about adding their signatures.

Although very beautiful works were sent by ship to Italy, the sculptors still reserved their finest products for their own city, creating the reputation of a beautiful city of marble that persisted until the Renaissance. The seamen who sailed round the ports of the Eastern Mediterranean buying ancient statues for the aristocracy of Europe would hear tales of a lost city of Aphrodisias beyond the Toros Mountains.

Finally, in 1740, the English traveller Richard Pococke arrived here and produced a description of the ruins. Attention was drawn to the site by Charles Texier's visit in 1835, and in 1892 Osman Hamdi Bey, the Director of the Istanbul Archaeological Museum, paid a visit to the site and decided on excavations, but the project never materialised. In the excavations conducted by the French archaeologists Gaudin and

Mendel in the years 1904-1913 and by the Italian archaeologist Jacopi in 1937 work was largely concentrated on the Baths of Hadrian and the Agora. At the beginning of the 20th century the city still remained almost entirely buried under the soil. The city walls, destroyed in the 7th century and never repaired, were in a state of complete ruin and the theatre was completely filled with earth, with the result that the site presented the appearance of an absolutely natural, untouched mound. Slender marble columns emerged here and there from amidst the poplars but when viewed from a distance, they could scarcely be distinguished from the tree trunks surrounding them.

A strange village by the name of Geyre grew up over and around the ruins. Although only 160 km from Izmir, its distance from the main road made it a place that very few people ever visited.

In 1956 the region was shaken by an earthquake which destroyed more than half of the houses in the village, upon which the authorities took advantage of the occasion to rebuild the village at a distance of about 2 km beyond the ancient site. During this resettlement process the villagers continued with the construction of a water channel from the skirts of the Babadağ Mt. and, in carrying out the excavations for the channel, their spades turned up some exquisite marble carvings and reliefs. This led to an invasion of the region by archaeologists who succeeded in persuading the villagers to choose a different route for their channel but, in spite of the manifest archaeological interest of the site, they merely erected a wire fence around the ruins and departed.

Aphrodisias still had to wait for some time for its name to become known.

Two years later, the famous

Aphrodisias, east-end of the pool in front of Tiberius Portico and Hadrianus Baths.

Aphrodisias, Hadrianus Baths.

photographer and traveller Ara Güler arrived in the nearby town of Aydın. Güler prefers villages to country towns, so after he had completed his business in Aydın he set out to find a village in which to spend the night.

"Chance took me to Geyre," he says, "I had never heard of the place in my life and when I saw it I really couldn't believe my eyes. Exquisite columns standing there. Statues of breathtaking beauty. Columns lying around on the ground - some of them used to prop up the precarious walls of village houses that seemed ready to collapse at any moment. One beautifully carved sarcophagus lid was being used as the trough of a village fountain while on another villagers were playing cards. I had never seen such an interesting place. I rushed off to get my camera and took a whole pile of photographs."

Güler later sent the pictures to his agent in Paris, who sent them to Horizon... The magazine asked for more, and Güler went back to Geyre to take them. But this time they wanted an explanatory text. Güler accordingly applied to the Istanbul Archaeological Museum. The Director told him he himself would not be able to help him but recommended an acquaintance of his in America. This acquaintance was Kenan Erim, an American of Turkish origin who was then Professor of Classical Archaeology in the University of New York. Kenan Erim had never visited Aphrodisias but he knew all about it. Ever since his student days in Princeton he had dreamed of Aphrodisias and how one day it might be his. After an initial visit in 1959 he returned to Aphrodisias in 1961 to embark on excavation work on the promise of financial assistance from the National Geographic. This excavation work, which was to occupy him for the rest of his life, further assisted

by various institutions such as the Andrew W. Mellon Foundation, the Vincent Astor Foundation and the Ford Foundation, combined with the arrangement of special tours. With the arrival of Kenan Erim, Aphrodisias took on a new lease of life. But for an archaeologist the discovery of Aphrodisias was a tremendous stroke of luck. None of the other excavations being carried on in Turkey in the field of classical archaeology yielded such a wealth of finds in so short a time. Indeed, fortune shone on Kenan Erim from the very first days. The trench dug by the peasants five years previously revealed remains of the city defence walls and towers as well as the head of a goddess. With this head in his hand Kenan Erim went straight to the hut containing the statues unearthed by the archaeologists who had dug there fifty years before, and here he succeeded in finding the torso to which the head belonged. It

Parts of statues in the museum garden.

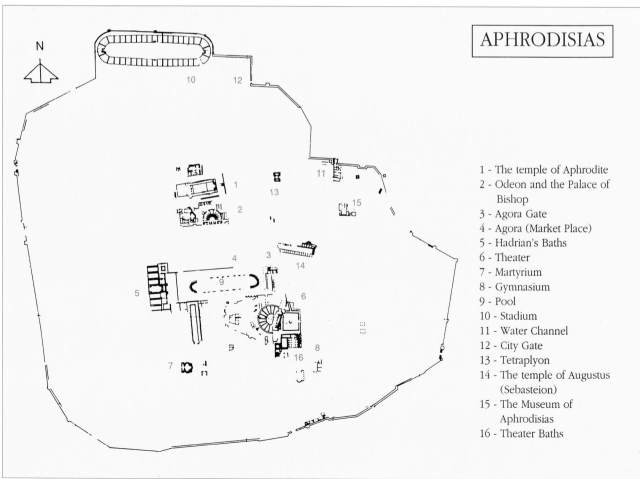

APHRODISIAS

1 - The temple of Aphrodite
2 - Odeon and the Palace of Bishop
3 - Agora Gate
4 - Agora (Market Place)
5 - Hadrian's Baths
6 - Theater
7 - Martyrium
8 - Gymnasium
9 - Pool
10 - Stadium
11 - Water Channel
12 - City Gate
13 - Tetraplyon
14 - The temple of Augustus (Sebasteion)
15 - The Museum of Aphrodisias
16 - Theater Baths

fitted exactly. It was as if this statue, created 1,700 years ago, had come back to life.

The same day, another miracle occurred. The caretaker found an inscribed piece of marble behind one of the cases left behind the hut. This also fitted exactly on to one side of the statue. On the fragment was the word "polis" (city). They had found the city on the very first day. They took this as a good omen. On the last day of the 1970 excavations they found "the people" in the theatre - a statue representing the people. Kenan Erim worked for thirty years at Aphrodisias, until his death in 1990. His grave lies in front of the Tetrapylon, the monumental gate of the cult centre of Aphrodite. Very great progress has been made in the excavations at Aphrodisias and the site has now been made more easily accessible, making it one of the most popular tourist attractions in Central-Western Anatolia.

THE RUINS
THE CITY DEFENCE WALLS AND CITY PLAN

The first thing you see on approaching Aphrodisias from the direction of Karacasu will be the city walls with the Ionic columns of the temple of Aphrodite in the background. The ancient city is located on a level piece of ground inclining slightly towards the south-west.

The construction of the walls is thought to have been begun during the Gothic invasion in 260, but the walls to be seen today date from the 4th century or later. No trace has been found of any defence system of an older date, but there may well have been a wall around the acropolis in the area between the agora and the theatre.

After the destruction of the walls by earthquake in the 7th century a fortress or observation tower was built here on the

highest point in the city. This was one of the first two areas of settlement. Of the two excavation zones yielding prehistoric remains one is located on this hill, on which a fortress or observation tower was built in the 7th century, and the other of the site occupied by the temple of Aphrodite.

The ancient acropolis was located on a hill 24 m high affording a view of the whole city.

The remains found here indicate the existence of a settlement in prehistoric times with seven separate layers identified as belonging to the bronze and iron ages. Traces have been found here of mudbrick walls on stone foundations and architectural structures reminiscent of megaron type houses.

Here too were found fairly large jars known as pithoi used for the storage of wheat and other provisions as well as a considerable amount of pottery fragments. The finds also include a number of stone implements, stone statuettes, figures with the faces of owls and fat female idols as well as various weight-measuring instruments.

The excavation area known as Pekmez Höyük to the east of the acropolis yielded pottery of the late neolithic, late chalcolithic and early bronze ages, together with two Kilia figurines.

In the Late Hellenistic period the city developed more particularly in the area surrounding the agora. There is no question, however, of any genuine town planning. Neither the Temple of Aphrodite nor the Sebastion conforms to any regular city plan.

Aphrodisias, general view of Agora and Hadrianus Baths.

Aphrodisias,
Aphrodite
Temple.

THE TEMPLE OF APHRODITE

Located in the northern section, in ancient times the Temple of Aphrodite formed the centre and nucleus of the city. All that remains of the ancient temple consists of fourteen of the over forty Ionic columns that once surrounded it and the foundations of the cella section. Although the cult centre dates back to earlier times the temple whose remains we see today was begun in the 1st century B.C. and is thought to have been completed during the reign of Augustus. The temenos (temple precinct) was completed in the 2nd century during the reign of Hadrian. The building would appear to have been what is known as an octastyle temple with thirteen columns on each side and eight columns at front and rear. On some of the columns are inscribed the names of the donors who presented them to the temple. The discovery of several mosaic fragments belonging to the Hellenistic period indicate the existence of an older temple on the same site, but with the conversion of the temple to a church in the 5th century all traces of the older building were erased. At the same time, the walls of the cella containing the cult statues were removed and the building enlarged by moving the side columns outwards. Walls were added at the front and rear of the building to form an apse and nave. An apse and an atrium were added on the east and west. No cult statue was found in the cella but in 1962 a statue was found immediately outside it bearing all the characteristics of a cult statue. This statue, which is now exhibited in the museum, displays a stiff, hieratic stance closely resembling the Artemis of Ephesus. The goddess is wearing a long

garment. One of the arms is stretched forward. The reliefs carved on the bands of the garment are very interesting. The sun god and moon goddess, the Three Graces with Aphrodite in the middle, Aphrodite and three Cupids seated on a goat with the tail of a fish are all symbols which frequently appear on various copies of the cult statue.

TETRAPYLON

One of the most attractive features of Aphrodisias is the ornamental gate constructed in the middle of the 2nd century. The name Tetrapylon refers to its being composed of four groups of four columns. The entrance lies to the east. The front row of Corinthian columns with spiral fluting look out on to a street with north-south alignment. The second and third columns of this fourfold structure are surmounted by a semicircular lintel with relief figures of Nike and Erotes amid acanthus leaves. The process of repairing and re-erecting the Tetrapylon columns was completed in 1990.

ODEON AND BISHOP'S PALACE

The odeon, a building which differed from the theatre in being used mainly as a concert hall and lecture room, is in a fairly good state of preservation.

Located immediately to the south of the temple, it was constructed in the 2nd century A.D. There were originally a larger number of tiers in the upper part of the buildings but these are thought to have been destroyed in an earthquake.

The orchestra and stage building of the odeon were adorned with mosaics and statues now preserved in the museum and

Aphrodisias, Aphrodite Temple.

Aphrodisias, Tetraphylon.

64

the auditorium was covered with a wooden roof. A fairly large architectural complex is to be found to the west of the odeon. Constructed in the Late Roman period, part of this building is thought to have later been used in the Byzantine period as the residence of a governor or bishop. It would thus appear that the temple and its environs preserved its status as a religious and administrative centre into Christian times.

A G O R A

The agora, located between the temple and the acropolis was planned in the 1st century B.C. for use as a market and popular meeting place. It is composed of two Ionic porticoes over 200 m long and running from east to west. The southern portico, which is known as the portico of Tiberius, was systematically examined in the course of the older excavations, while the 1937 excavations carried out by the Italian team yielded extremely valuable friezes together with inscriptions written in praise of the Emperor Tiberius.

Recent excavations conducted in the northern section, in the western section near the baths of Hadrian and the gate of the agora in the south-east yielded a large number of very fine specimens of the skill of the Aphrodisian sculptors and stone-carvers. Most of the reliefs consist of sacred or individual portraits surrounded by wreaths or garlands, masks and mythological scenes.

The monumental gate of the agora is located at the eastern end of the Portico of Tiberius. This ornamental entrance was erected in the middle of the 2nd century but in order to prevent the flooding that followed the 4th century earthquake it was converted into a nymphaeum and connected to a water supply system to be

Aphodisias, Odeon.

used in controlling the water flow.

This is thought to have been constructed in the 5th century and to have suffered severe damage in the 7th century earthquake. Among the scenes represented on the reliefs in the niches on the Agora gate are to be seen the struggle between the Centaurs and the Lapiths (Centauromachy), between the Gods and the Giants (Gigantomachy) and between the Amazons and the Greeks (Amazonomachy).

BATHS OF HADRIAN

The baths constructed in the 2nd century during the reign of the Emperor Hadrian lie to the west of the Portico of Tiberius. This complex consists of a large central hall, probably the caldarium or hot room, surrounded by four large rooms, the tepidarium, sudatorium, apoditerium and frigidarium (warm room, sweating room, dressing room and cold room respectively).

Aphodisias, Palace of the Bishop.

It is a most imposing building with all the requisite facilities, such as labyrinthine underground service corridors, water channels and furnaces.

In the excavations conducted here in 1904 the French archaeologist Paul Gaudin unearthed a large number of artistic works now preserved in the Istanbul Archaeological Museum.

THEATRE

Begun in 1966, the excavations in the theatre area yielded a great deal of extremely valuable information regarding both the prehistoric and historic periods in Aphrodisias as well as very well preserved sections of the theatre building and a large number of statues and reliefs of the highest quality.

The theatre building rests against the eastern slope of the acropolis. Construction was completed in 27 B.C. but in the 2nd century A.D. certain structural changes were

made to make the theatre suitable for gladiatorial combats. The stage building was enlarged and connected to the cavea, a room for the wild animals was opened in the rear and some corridors were added.

Following the collapse of the upper sections of the cavea in the 7th century earthquake and the partial filling up of the auditorium the Byzantine inhabitants covered the orchestra and stage buildings with earth and built houses over it, at the same time surrounding the acropolis with a wall.The most interesting and remarkable of the finds discovered in the excavations was the Zoilos relief. Zoilos was a manumitted slave of Octavian who played an influential rôle in fostering good relations between Aphrodisias and Rome and who succeeded in having the city exempted from tax. The proscenion and logeion sections of the theatre were presented by Zoilos as a gift to Aphrodite and the citizens of Aphrodisias.

SEBASTION

The Sebastion is a most remarkable discovery, not only as regards the excavations in Aphrodisias but in the whole context of classical archaeological excavation. When the building was first unearthed in 1979 it appeared to have no relation to any other building but, as excavations were carried down to deeper levels, it became apparent that this consisted of a temple dedicated to the cult of the Emperor Augustus (Sebastos is the Greek equivalent of the Latin Augustus) and its surrounding complex.

Of the temple only the foundations now remain, together with a few column bases, Corinthian style capitals and architrave blocks. In addition to the damage inflicted by the earthquakes in the 4th and 7th centuries, the remains of the temple also suffered from the use of the area for

Aphrodisias, Sebastion.

Aphrodisias, Stadium, it is the most splendid stage Stadium in Anatolia.

settlement in the Byzantine and Turkish periods.

The temple, which was located at the eastern end of the Sebastion, consisted of two porticoes 80 m in length composed of half columns and a ceremonial way 14 m wide. At the western end there was a gate or propylon opening on to the street. Excavations both inside and outside the porticoes yielded a quite extraordinary quantity of reliefs and decorative panels. The most remarkable of these included depictions of the birth of Eros, the Three Graces, Apollo in Delphi, Meleager, Achilles and Penthesilea, Nyssa and the child Dionysus. There are also reliefs of some members of the imperial family and mythological figures. Those identitifed include Augustus, Germanicus, Lucius, Gaius Caesar, Claudius and Agrippa, together with Prometheus and Aeneas fleeing from Troy. There is also a

particularly interesting group of reliefs symbolizing Claudius's conquest of Britain and Nero's conquest of Armenia.

There are also a number of fragments depicting the peoples of the various countries with which Augustus had waged war or formed other types of relationships but these have suffered severe earthquake damage.

It would appear from the epigraphic evidence that the Sebastion porticoes were built during the reigns of Claudius and Nero and were the gifts of two separate families.

STADIUM

The Aphrodisias stadium is the best preserved of all the ancient stadiums in the Mediterranean region. Located in the northern section of the city it is 262 m in length and 59 m wide with a seating capacity of 30,000. The ends of the stadium

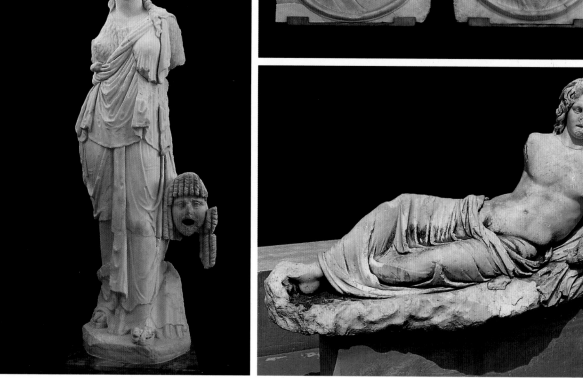

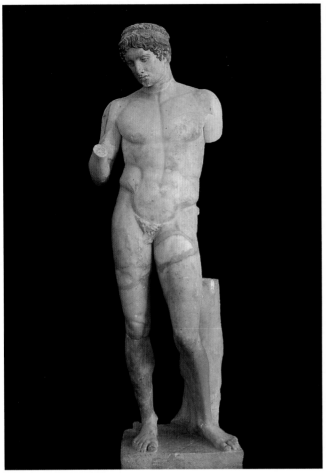

Views from Aphrodisias Museum.

Melpomone, statue of tragedy Muse.

Statue of Flavius Palmatus.

From the museum garden, sarcophagus with god reliefs.

Marble portraits.

Zoilos relief, general view.

are slightly convex, giving the whole a form rather suggesting an ellipse. In this way, the spectators seated in this part of the stadium would not block each other's view and would be able to see the whole of the arena.

The stadium was specially designed for athletic contests, but after the theatre was damaged in the 7th century earthquake the eastern end of the arena began to be used for games, circuses and wild beast shows. During the Roman period the stadium was the scene of a large number of athletic competitions and festivals.

These competitions in the province of Asia Minor were modelled on the Olympic and Pythian games in Greece, and had the same name and organization as the Greek equivalent.

These shows were held with the permission of Rome and the granting of such permission was regarded as a signal

honour. The games held in Aphrodisias were Pythian, not Olympic. These were complemented by the Gordineia festivals held in honour of the Emperor and with his special permission.

THE MUSEUM OF APHRODISIAS

The Museum of Aphrodisias is one of the most outstanding museums of western Anatolia. The monuments of unsurpassed value which have been found at the excavations are displayed here.

Observing these finds and imagining them in their former places suffice to grasp the splendor of these antique monuments which once used to be. Especially the works of the sculpture school of antique Aphrodisias show the level of development of this art.

PAMUKKALE
HIERAPOLIS-APHRODISIAS

CONTENTS